Jean Tong is a Naarm-based writer, dramaturg, director, and Associate Artist with Melbourne Theatre Company. For theatre, Jean's writing credits include: the critically acclaimed *Flat Earthers: The Musical* (Griffin Theatre Company/Hayes Theatre co); *Hungry Ghosts* (Melbourne Theatre Company); and Green Room award nominee *Romeo is Not the Only Fruit*. Their directing work includes *Dying: A Memoir* (Melbourne Theatre Company); *Caught* (Red Stitch Actors' Theatre) and *Oh No! Satan Stole My Pineal Gland!* (Melbourne Fringe). For screen, Jean's writing credits include *Heartbreak High* S2 (Netflix/Fremantle), *Safe Home* (SBS/Kindling Pictures), *Erotic Stories* (SBS/Lingo Pictures), and *100% Wolf* S2 (ABC). They were the script co-ordinator for *New Gold Mountain* (SBS/Goalpost) and are currently developing original works for film and television with Photoplay, SBS and Screen Australia. Jean was the inaugural 2023 Melbourne Theatre Company NEXT STAGE Fellow, and the Belvoir St Theatre Philip Parsons Writing Fellow in 2020. In 2025, Jean was selected by Australians in Film and Screen Australia to take part in their Talent Gateway program.

DO NOT PASS GO

By Jean Tong

CURRENCY PRESS
The performing arts publisher

MELBOURNE THEATRE COMPANY

CURRENT THEATRE SERIES

First published in 2026
by Currency Press Pty Ltd,
Gadigal Land, Suite 310, 46–56 Kippax Street, Surry Hills, NSW 2010, Australia
enquiries@currency.com.au
www.currency.com.au

in association with Melbourne Theatre Company

Typeset by Brighton Gray for Currency Press.
Printed by Fineline Print + Copy Services, Revesby, NSW.
Cover shows Belinda McClory and Ella Prince. Cover design by Sarah Ridgway-Cross.

Currency Press acknowledges the Traditional Owners of the Country on which we live and work. We pay our respects to all Aboriginal and Torres Strait Islander Elders, past and present.

A catalogue record for this book is available from the National Library of Australia

Contents

Belinda McClory in rehearsal (Photo: Matto Lucas)

Composer & Sound Designer Marco Cher and Director Katy Maudlin in rehearsal (Photo: Matto Lucas)

Author's Note

I started my playwriting residency at Melbourne Theatre Company in 2023 with high hopes. I was going to write it. You know it. The one that tumbles out when you know what you want to say and exactly how to say it. It's the one you get the full commission for because you've like, proved you're a real writer. I was finally going to do it. I was going to write *The Play*.

Yeah, nah. I spent a year wandering Melbourne Theatre Company HQ trying and failing to answer everyone's questions about *The Play*. I started three different plays. I accepted online invitations to quarterly meetings and all-staff events, and I was repeatedly moved by the infinite energy being poured into a workplace whose fundamental aim is creating ephemeral experiences that outlast and outshine us.

My colleagues sustained me, encouraging my haunted spectre, despite how often I drifted through the hallways complaining about writer's block. I kept working. I took the title from my third unfinished (mediocre) play; the character names from my second nearly finished (fine) play; and the themes from my first (thankfully unfinished) play.

And here we are. It's not *The Play*. But it's the play I wanted to write. It's the play I didn't think I would get to write, and it's the play I'm most grateful to have had the freedom to finish.

In a time of intense work pressure and the expectation of constant output, I was privileged to be given enough time to *not* work, in order to work *well*.

These ideas drive *Do Not Pass Go*, undermining the outside world's insistence that constant work is fair trade for living in an age of convenience. We are sold this as universal even though in our bones, we know the truth: for most, there is less time and less money than ever before.

And yet we work.

But what if we didn't?

Ella Prince in rehearsal (Photo: Matto Lucas)

Ella Prince, Belinda McClory, Stage Manager Pippa Wright and Director Katy Maudlin in rehearsal (Photo: Matto Lucas)

Acknowledgements

Do Not Pass Go would not exist without the encouragement, engagement, and meandering I got to do with Zoey Dawson, Jennifer Medway, Mark Wilson, Tasnim Hossain, and Anne-Louise Sarks at Melbourne Theatre Company. Thank you for believing me (or at least pretending to) every time I proclaimed that my latest brainchild was definitely, absolutely, for real this time, *The Play*.

I am happily and permanently in a great deal of debt to the cast and creative team, in particular director Katy Maudlin and actors Belinda McClory and Ella Prince. Your commitment to this work is astounding, and your belief in the play made it real. You are my favourite forever shirts.

To Shonie—thank you for reminding me to lie flat, and for lying flat with me. Love you.

Lighting Designer Harrie Hogan in rehearsal (Photo: Matto Lucas)

Writer Jean Tong in rehearsal (Photo: Matto Lucas)

Do Not Pass Go was first presented by Melbourne Theatre Company at Southbank Theatre, The Lawler, Melbourne, on the lands of the Boon Wurrung and Wurundjeri Woi Wurrung peoples of the Kulin Nation, on 14 February 2026 with the following cast and creatives:

PENNY	Belinda McClory
FLUX	Ella Prince

Director, Katy Maudlin
Set & Costume Designer, Jacob Battista
Lighting Designer, Harrie Hogan
Composer & Sound Designer, Marco Cher
Intimacy Coordinator, Amy Cater
Stage Manager, Pippa Wright
Assistant Stage Manager, Jenny Le

Melbourne Theatre Company acknowledges the Boon Wurrung and Wurundjeri Woi Wurrung peoples of the Kulin Nation, the Traditional Custodians of the land on which we work, create and gather. We pay our respects to all First Nations people, their Elders past and present, and their enduring connections to Country, knowledge, and stories. As a Company we remain committed to the invitation of the Uluru Statement from the Heart and its call for voice, truth and treaty.

NEXTSTAGE

Commissioned and developed through Melbourne Theatre Company's NEXT STAGE Writers' Program, with the support of our Playwrights Giving Circle.

CHARACTERS

FLUX, wants things to change (they think)

PENNY, doesn't (she thinks)

SPACE

Flux and Penny are in an almost-recognisable period of late-stage capitalism, at a workplace largely encompassing repetitive, banal tasks.

Their work is everything. Their work is how they escape each other and themselves. It is the subtext and the text. It is a welcome distraction and a terrible burden. It is whatever they need it to be. It is not enough.

Some moments of work are included as an indication of rhythm. These are not prescriptive or comprehensive. Each production is welcome to discover their own work rhythm.

Another prompt, not a rule: once we're in the space, we don't leave. Until we do.

This playtext went to press before the end of rehearsals and may differ from the play as performed.

ACT ONE

FIRST DAY

FLUX *arrives.*

PENNY *pauses her work.*

PENNY: You must be—
FLUX: Flux.
PENNY: Flux? They said they hired someone called—
FLUX: I prefer Flux.
PENNY: You're late.
FLUX: I had to be inducted. They couldn't get my pass working.
PENNY: We'd better get started or we'll fall behind.
FLUX: Is it just us?
PENNY: Yes. You have what you need?

FLUX *holds up their uniform.*

If you put that on, we can start.
FLUX: Small department.
PENNY: A lot of people got made redundant last year.
FLUX: Then you needed more help?
PENNY: I don't. But they wanted more output, faster.
FLUX: Lucky me.
PENNY: You've done this before?
FLUX: Yeah.
I've assisted.
PENNY: Right. Shall we—
FLUX: What was your name?
PENNY: … Penny.
FLUX: Looking forward to working with you, Penny.
PENNY: Have you watched the compliance videos? You can't work until you do.
FLUX: What compliance videos?
PENNY: It's on the portal. You'll have to log in first.

FLUX *tries to log in.*

FLUX: It says login error.

PENNY: First name dot last name.

FLUX: I did that.

PENNY: It's case sensitive.

FLUX: Why?

PENNY: Not my department.

FLUX *tries again. They succeed.*

PENNY*, smug, starts working again.*

The videos will pop up first thing when you open the staff portal.

FLUX: It's not working.

PENNY: Why not?

FLUX: It says I don't exist. Where's IT?

PENNY: They're offsite. You have to log a job via the portal.

FLUX: What about the people who fixed my pass?

PENNY: That's maintenance. They can't help you.

FLUX: Right.

PENNY: Did you put your name in correctly?

FLUX: Isn't it the same as the login?

PENNY: The portal is first *initial* and last name.

FLUX *tries it.*

FLUX: Maybe they haven't set up my employee profile.

PENNY: They will have. Or you wouldn't have been able to get onsite.

FLUX: Can't you log a job for me?

PENNY: Did you use a dot?

FLUX: Yes, I know how to log in—

PENNY: No dot for the portal. First initial last name.

They try it. They don't say anything.

Did it work?

FLUX: Yes.

PENNY: Did the compliance videos come up?

FLUX: Yes.

PENNY: You can change the speed, but the next page won't load until the length of the video's passed. So there's no point. It's the same for the emergency procedure video. Once you've finished that, I'll get you to assist me.

FLUX: Fine.

This might take a while.

PENNY: They should've gotten you to do this before you started.

FLUX: Yeah, I got an email about it.

PENNY: Why didn't you complete it?

FLUX: I hadn't started.

FLUX *starts watching the video on full volume.*

PENNY *tries to keep working but she is unsettled.*

FLUX, *bored, watches the videos with great inattention.*

PENNY*'s phone buzzes. She doesn't look at it.*

FLUX *looks over, curious.*

PENNY*'s phone vibrates with a call.* PENNY *ignores it.*

I think your phone is ringing.

PENNY: Yes.

PENNY *lets the phone ring out.*

FLUX: You're not going to pick up?

PENNY: No.

FLUX: Who is it?

PENNY: Sorry, it's just, if I lose focus I can't get it back and then it'll be the end of the day and I won't have done what I need to do.

FLUX: Oh, ADHD, sorry.

PENNY: Excuse me?

FLUX: No, I get it. My dad used to yell at us when we went into his office without knocking because he'd 'go off-track and never get back on again'.

PENNY: That's awful.

FLUX: He was undiagnosed.

PENNY: Right. And there's nothing wrong with—it—that. But this is just how I do it; once I start, I'm in. That's all.

FLUX: Sorry. I won't interrupt.

PENNY: I'll turn it off.

FLUX: You can answer, I won't listen.

PENNY: We shouldn't do personal calls at work.

PENNY *keeps working. But she's distracted.*

FLUX *keeps watching compliance videos.*

WORK SPACE 1

FLUX: Morning.
PENNY: You're late.

PENNY *is disapproving.*

Why don't you start on this?

PENNY *gives* FLUX *an unnervingly simple task.*

FLUX: Really?
PENNY: Someone's got to do it.

FLUX *starts.*

PENNY *does something extremely specific to help herself focus, and then starts a more complex task.*

They don't say anything else to each other.

BABY STEPS

FLUX: Do you want a coffee?

PENNY: No, thank you.

FLUX: Tea?

PENNY: No.

FLUX: Okay.

PENNY *works.* FLUX *procrastinates.*

Do you like it?

PENNY: What?

FLUX: This. Here.

PENNY: Yes.

FLUX: It's a little …

PENNY: What?

FLUX: Nothing.

They work.

So we just do this?

PENNY: Yes.

FLUX: Kinda weird.

PENNY: That's work.

FLUX: I guess.

I thought there'd be more people. Someone looking over our shoulder.

PENNY: They don't need to, if we do this well.

FLUX: Does anyone actually care?

PENNY: I do.

FLUX: Right.

They work.

The pay's good.

PENNY: It's a good job.

FLUX: I needed something more consistent.

PENNY: It's a good, permanent job.

FLUX: Except for the redundancies.

PENNY: Well. No-one's permanent.

FLUX *gets bored. They stop working.*

FLUX: Can I be honest?

PENNY: Are you asking?

FLUX: It feels pointless.

PENNY: It's not.

FLUX: Couldn't they automate this?

PENNY: Not yet.

If they did, they wouldn't need us. Don't you want this?

FLUX: I need this.

But I wanted to do something more …

PENNY: More what?

FLUX: More … *More*.

I used to think I'd do something useful, like put out bushfires somewhere rural.

PENNY: Isn't that a volunteer position?

FLUX: It's just an example.

They work.

PENNY: Every job means something. A job is a series of tasks and we live to get things done. Would you rather be back in the fields or the mines?

FLUX: A lot of people are.

PENNY: If we weren't productive we would lose our minds and go back to being Neanderthals. It's a privilege to be productive.

You said you needed this job?

FLUX: Yes.

PENNY: So you're here for a reason. What's more meaningful than that?

WEEKEND

FLUX *yawns. Looks at the time. Starts packing up.*

FLUX: Think I'm done.
PENNY: You've finished?
FLUX: Done for the week.
PENNY: Enjoy your weekend.
FLUX: Any plans tonight?
PENNY: The usual.

FLUX *waits.*

Get home. Make dinner. Family. You know.
FLUX: You have kids?
PENNY: One.

FLUX *waits.*

She's fifteen.

FLUX *waits.*

She gets stressed if I'm home late. So I'd better get through this.
FLUX: Of course.

FLUX *lingers.*

PENNY: You? Any plans?
FLUX: Nah, I should go as well. My partner will want to watch *Real Housewives*. Maybe open a rosé. Zone out. Do you watch it?
PENNY: I don't watch TV. If I sit down in front of the TV, that's it. I'm asleep.
FLUX: I'm the same. Yeah. I get home and I'm wiped, I don't know how you do it.
PENNY: It's simple.
FLUX: Is it?
PENNY: It's easy to be good at this.

FLUX *lingers.*

FLUX: Sometimes I dream about being back here. Do you?
PENNY: I don't dream.

PENNY*'s phone vibrates. She ignores it. Keeps working.*

FLUX: Well. Goodnight.
PENNY: Goodnight.

LUNCH 1

PENNY *demonstrates to* FLUX *a series of exercises designed to combat the physical stress of the job they do.* FLUX *copies* PENNY *as best they can.*

FLUX: Should this be a compulsory part of lunch?
PENNY: It helps prevent various potential workplace-induced physical harms like RSI.
FLUX: But should it be during our lunch hour?
PENNY: When else would it be?
FLUX: During work?
PENNY: Why would we do this during work? That's not part of the job.
FLUX: It is if it reduces potential workplace-induced physical harms.
PENNY: That's not their responsibility.
FLUX: It's their workplace.
PENNY: But then we'd spend less time on work.
FLUX: But this is work.
PENNY: This isn't work. This is self-improvement.
FLUX: To support our work.
PENNY: If you say so. I like the routine.
FLUX: Maybe I should ask if we can do this during work hours.
PENNY: They'll say no.
FLUX: We could refuse to work.

PENNY *laughs and starts eating a muesli bar and goes back to work. It's the first time* FLUX *has heard* PENNY *laugh.*

FLUX *opens a packet of chips. They tuck the corners of the packet in to create a bowl, making it easier to get at the chips. It's a particularly noisy and time-consuming process.* PENNY *cannot bear it.*

FLUX *sees* PENNY *watching and offers her a chip.*

PENNY: No thank you.
Make sure your hands are clean before you continue.

They work.

ICEBREAKER

They work. They're more in sync.

PENNY: It's a bit odd.
FLUX: Hm?
PENNY: Having someone around all the time. Again.
FLUX: Mm. Yeah.
PENNY: Bit odd.
FLUX: How many people used to work here?
PENNY: It used to be three, then it was six, and then it was four, now it's just me. And you.
FLUX: This is pretty quiet for me.
PENNY: Right. Retail?
FLUX: Bartending. But yeah.

They work.

Do you keep up with the people who left?
PENNY: Who?
FLUX: Your colleagues. The ones who got made redundant.
PENNY: Not really. We just worked together. Do you?
FLUX: Sometimes. We're friends.
PENNY: You must have a lot of those.

They work.

FLUX: Apparently three. The average number of friends adults have. Well. Three point six. I read that somewhere. Kind of sad.
PENNY: I feel like having three point six friends is good.
FLUX: It's better than having no friends.
PENNY: Can you name three point six?
FLUX: Yeah, easy.

PENNY *counts in her head. Comes up short.*

They work.

PENNY: How do *you* define that?
FLUX: Hm?
PENNY: Friend.
FLUX: Oh. Uh. I guess someone you'd call in an emergency.

PENNY: I'd probably call family.

FLUX: Okay, no. People you actually want to talk to.
If you had to call someone on *Who Wants To Be A Millionaire?*, who would you call?

PENNY: People often call family.

FLUX: Not everyone.

They work.

A friend is someone who knows your birthday and shows up with cake unannounced.

PENNY: Sounds inconvenient.

FLUX: I guess.

PENNY: You must get a lot of unannounced cakes.

FLUX: Not really.

They work.

PENNY: The other day, you said partner?

FLUX: Yeah, my boyfriend.

PENNY: Really?!

FLUX: What?

PENNY: A boyfriend? That's so unexpected. Sorry, not because you're not—it's more that I didn't think you—how did you meet him?

FLUX: Them.

PENNY: Them. How did you meet them?

FLUX: We met at a lesbian rave under a bridge.

PENNY: Oh.

FLUX: I was vomiting in a bush and they got me a bottle of water.

PENNY: So.
Your boyfriend is a lesbian.

FLUX: Yes.

PENNY: And they …

FLUX: Yes?

PENNY: Are they a—
Are they are a girl-they or a boy-they?

FLUX: That's not how that works.

PENNY: No?

FLUX: No.

PENNY: No.

That's a lovely way to meet. In person. The way people used to.

FLUX: Yeah.

Long pause.

Girl-they.

They work.

They just talk about work when we hang out. My friends from work. Sometimes I feel like I have nothing to talk to them about.

PENNY: I think that's normal. With work friends.

FLUX: Yeah. I guess they're just work friends.

They work.

REVIEW

FLUX *is late.*

PENNY: Morning.
FLUX: Morning.
PENNY: Slow start.
FLUX: I was upstairs.
PENNY: Why?
FLUX: Probation review.
PENNY: Oh!

FLUX *starts working.*

PENNY: How was it?
FLUX: Fine.

PENNY *waits.*

PENNY: That's good.

PENNY *waits.*

FLUX: They said I need to be more productive.
PENNY: Ah.
FLUX: And I need to stop being late.
PENNY: The hours are the hours.
Did they say anything else?
FLUX: How do you do it?
PENNY: Me?
FLUX: You just churn through. Just show up every day and churn through.
PENNY: Sometimes it's hard.

PENNY *does the extremely specific thing she does to make herself go back to work.*

FLUX: I feel like you really care.
PENNY: I like doing a good job.
FLUX: I should try that.
And sorry for distracting you.
PENNY: You're not distracting me.

FLUX: They said that my arrival has resulted in general productivity dipping even if overall productivity has gone up.

PENNY: What?

FLUX: We're getting more done, but less than we should.

PENNY: That's not good.

FLUX: They said maybe the training was taking up too much time.

PENNY: They said that?

FLUX: But it's me. I'm the problem.

PENNY: It's not your fault. You're still learning. I mean, you shouldn't be, but you are and that's fine. It's fine. It happens.

FLUX: I don't want to lose this job. I can't lose this job.

PENNY: You won't.

FLUX: What if I don't get better at this?

PENNY: You will. You just have to focus.
Okay? Let's get to work.

FLUX: Okay.

LUNCH 2

PENNY *does the workplace physical exercises to combat workplace-related physical stress.*

FLUX *is on their phone.*

FLUX: 'Only through lying flat can humans become the measure of all things … '

PENNY: I beg your pardon?

FLUX: Some guy in China posted his manifesto on a forum. He couldn't take the pressure of the city so he moved back to the country. He says he just eats enough to live and works enough to eat. And the rest of the time … 'I can live like Diogenes and sleep inside a wooden bucket.'

PENNY: So he's dropped out of society?

FLUX: He's still online.

PENNY: Don't they have ninety percent home ownership there?

FLUX: What does that have to do with anything?

PENNY: Of course he can lie down.

FLUX: I think it's cool.

PENNY: Giving up on the world?

FLUX: He hasn't given up on the world. He's given up on work.

PENNY: I earned my ability to work.

FLUX: I guess he wants the ability to not work.

PENNY: It's a waste. If he can write a manifesto then he can get up and do something about it.

FLUX: I guess.

PENNY *finishes her exercises and keeps working.* FLUX, *quietly—*

'I choose to lie flat, and I am no longer afraid.'

WORK SPACE 2

PENNY, *at work, alone.*

She looks over to where FLUX *normally works.*

It's empty.

She keeps working.

She looks over again.

She stops.

Hesitates.

Keeps working.

Looks over.

Keeps working.

SICKIE

PENNY *arrives to find* FLUX *already at their desk, working.*

PENNY: You're back.

FLUX: Yep.

PENNY: Where were you?

FLUX: I took sick leave.

PENNY: Oh.

I've never used mine. I don't think I'd know how to submit a request.

FLUX: It's easy.

PENNY: I can't afford to use it.

They work.

If I took sick leave every time I got a sniffle or a cold or a flu, I wouldn't have anything left for a real emergency.

FLUX: So you come to work sick?

PENNY: I have to.

FLUX: But then you just spread it around.

PENNY: Do you think I got you sick?

FLUX: I didn't say that.

PENNY: Are you still sick?

FLUX: No.

PENNY: How bad was it?

FLUX: I couldn't stand doing this for eight hours.

PENNY: I'm glad you're back.

What was it?

FLUX: Just. Sick.

PENNY: Sorry, it's private. I'll stop prying.

They work.

FLUX: I took a mental health day.

PENNY: Oh.

I didn't know that was covered.

FLUX: I went fishing.

PENNY: That's definitely not covered.

FLUX: I couldn't sleep the night before. I was up until four a.m. next to my partner, trying to stay calm, trying not to wake them because they had work early the next day, trying to tell myself it didn't matter that the thought of coming in and doing this made me feel—

So I got in my car and I drove.

There's this spot, about two hours away. I sit and I watch the sun come up between the trees. It was so orange. The orangest thing I'd ever seen. And then I sent an email saying I was too sick to come in and I put a line down and listened to the leaves rustling and felt the water on my toes and my stomach and my chest and my face and I didn't catch anything all day and I got sunburnt and thirsty and bitten all over because I forgot to bring insect repellant and I didn't see a single person and it was the best day I've had in … in a long time.

That's where I was.

PENNY: I couldn't spend my leave on that.

I couldn't.

TEAM BUILDING

PENNY *opens a packet of chips. She thinks about turning it into a free-standing bowl. Maybe she even tries. But the fuss and noise put her off.*

She offers FLUX *a chip.*

FLUX: Thanks.
PENNY: You're welcome.

They work.

ACT TWO

WORK SPACE 3

FLUX *looks at how much work they have to get through.*

FLUX: Is there more than last time?
PENNY: No.
FLUX: I feel like there's more.
PENNY: It's always like that.
FLUX: Really?
PENNY: Don't worry. We'll get through it.

BELIEF

PENNY*'s phone vibrates. It breaks her focus.*

FLUX *yawns. They try to work.*

Both are in a weird inattentive state.

PENNY: Tired?
FLUX: My partner and I were out last night.
PENNY: Did you have fun?
FLUX: Nah. Got too drunk.
PENNY: Sounds fun.
FLUX: Not really.

Both of them try to work. It's lacklustre.

Ten minutes?
PENNY: Five.
FLUX: Eight.
PENNY: Six.
FLUX: Eight. I'll read your horoscope!
PENNY: I don't believe in horoscopes. But go on. I think I'm a—
FLUX: No, I know, don't worry, I know exactly—here you are. Okay. 'There's a strong urge for delusional joy, driven by power planet Pluto.'
PENNY: That doesn't sound right.
FLUX: 'Consider how you balance work and play. Do you feel valued at work? Or are you committing more than you have?'
PENNY: That's what it says?
FLUX: 'Create space for yourself. As the sun glints off Jupiter's rings, don't let anyone dull your sparkle.'
PENNY: Lots to consider.
FLUX: It's good. It's a good one.
PENNY: Do you believe in them? Horoscopes.
FLUX: Better than a non-existent god. Sorry, are you—do you believe in god? Are you religious?
PENNY: I was raised religious. But now I just ask God what to do when I'm looking at fourteen different types of milk.
FLUX: There's too many questions to not believe in *something*.

PENNY: Who doesn't like a confident answer?

FLUX: 'Don't dull your sparkle'.

PENNY: What does yours say?

FLUX *hesitates.*

I'm interested. Genuinely.

FLUX: It's fine, I don't want to read it again.

PENNY: Is it embarrassing?

FLUX: No, no …
'You'll know if it's time to cast off old burdens … '

FLUX *gets emotional.*

PENNY: Oh, uh—are you alright?

FLUX: It's just—I've been thinking about—sorry, it's stupid, we said eight minutes.

PENNY: No, you need to—do you want a tea?

FLUX: It's fine, sorry. I've just been feeling kind of. Like nothing makes sense anymore. It's all a bit—you know?

PENNY: Sure. Sure.

FLUX: And I think maybe it's because I might have to break up with my partner.

PENNY: Sorry?

FLUX: Because it could be a sign. *The* sign. Because sometimes the relationship feels like that, like a burden.

PENNY: So you think you should … cast off your partner?

FLUX: More like … conscious uncoupling.

PENNY: Is a horoscope the best way to make that decision?

FLUX: I'm not an idiot.

PENNY: No.

FLUX: But I was already thinking about it so it does feel like the universe trying to tell me something, right?

PENNY: I don't know, I don't know if I should say.

FLUX: Maybe I should get the paid app. So I can get more specific details.

PENNY: How much is the paid app?

FLUX: Twelve ninety-nine.

PENNY: That's not so bad.

FLUX: Per month.

PENNY: I guess there's not a *good* way to decide these things. Are there any signs other than the horoscope?

FLUX: They uh.

Asked if I wanted to adopt a dog.

PENNY: That's nice. Isn't it?

FLUX: But what does that *mean*? First it's 'what kind of dog?' then it's 'hey you know this dog would look so cute carrying our rings down the aisle', and then it's 'isn't this three-bedroom townhouse *so* charming?' and then it's 'this room is perfect for a nursery' next minute we're married with twins and rushing home every night to make dinner every night *every night* and we're tired so tired and we sit in front of the TV not talking not touching and we don't hate each other but do we like each other or are we just doing something we fell into because we thought it was what we wanted? Thinking about that, about that future, about doing that every day over and over and over makes me want to—

A beat.

PENNY: Sounds *terrible*.

FLUX: Sorry, that was rude, I didn't mean—

PENNY *checks her watch.*

They work.

I don't even know if that's what they want. But I panicked and said I didn't want to vacuum dog hair every day.

PENNY: What did they say?

FLUX: That we could buy a Roomba.

They work.

How did you know it was the right thing to do?

PENNY: What was?

FLUX: Starting a family.

PENNY: I didn't.

FLUX: Do you ever regret it?

PENNY: No.

FLUX: You're happy?

PENNY: I love my daughter.

FLUX: Good.

They work.

PENNY: I've been looking into it. The thing you said about your dad, the um, ADHD.

FLUX: Oh yeah?

PENNY: Yes.

It's interesting.

FLUX: Yeah?

PENNY: I've got an appointment. With a specialist.

FLUX: Oh good.

PENNY: So. We'll see.

PENNY *does the thing she does.*

SURGERY 1

They work. FLUX *stops* PENNY.

FLUX: No, it's easier like this.

PENNY: What?

FLUX: It's easier if you—

FLUX is right. It is easier.

PENNY: You're getting good at this.

FLUX: I guess.
I didn't think I'd be here long enough to get better.

PENNY: How long did you think you'd be here?

FLUX: Just long enough to save for surgery.

PENNY: Right, your—

FLUX: Yeah. I thought—just get in, get out, get it done. But I've had to push it, I'm on the bottom of the waitlist again.

PENNY: There's a waitlist?

FLUX: Yeah. It's expensive but there's still a long waitlist.

PENNY: I didn't know that many people wanted it.

FLUX: *And* I'll have to take time off to recover. This is the most regular money I've made but it just—goes. So I guess I'll be here longer than I planned.

PENNY: That's good. Not pushing the—I mean, I don't mind that you'll be here longer.

They work.

Can I ask you a question?

FLUX: Sure.

PENNY: I'm not saying you shouldn't.

FLUX: Shouldn't what?

PENNY: I just want to understand as best I can, as someone who doesn't feel the need to do this kind of thing to their body, to alter or or or—

FLUX: Yep.

PENNY: I don't want to come across judgmental, if you're thinking, 'I can't wait to tell people how judgmental she was' then I won't ask. I won't even ask.

FLUX: I'm not thinking that.

PENNY: So—

FLUX: Yeah?

PENNY: Why do you want this surgery?

FLUX: I think it will allow me to feel at home in my body.

PENNY: Right.

You don't feel that way right now?

FLUX: No. Never.

PENNY: Because you don't look the way—

FLUX: The way I feel. Right.

PENNY: Right.

FLUX: Does that make sense?

PENNY: Honestly? Not really. But it doesn't matter. I'm not the one getting it.

They work.

Do you think it's because—

FLUX: What?

PENNY: Well, do you think maybe you're taking so long because—actually, don't worry.

FLUX: No, say it.

PENNY: Maybe you're putting it off. Maybe you're subconsciously trying to give yourself more time to think about it.

FLUX: I'm doing my best.

PENNY: I'm not saying you're not. It's just a big decision.

FLUX: It's difficult to save.

PENNY: No, completely.

FLUX: And sometimes I have to spend money on other things. For life.

PENNY: Absolutely. I'm just saying—

FLUX: That I shouldn't get the surgery.

PENNY: That is absolutely not what—I'm sorry. Forget I said anything.

FLUX: It's fine if you think that.

PENNY: I really don't. I'm just wondering if *you,* subconsciously, maybe, because it's a big—anyway, don't—just, please, forget it. Forget my big mouth.

FLUX: I'm not subconsciously self-sabotaging.

PENNY: No.

FLUX: I'm not.

PENNY *works.*

FLUX *doesn't.*

DEFICIT

FLUX *works.*

PENNY *is trying to. But it's hard today.*

PENNY: My appointment's next week.
FLUX: Oh, for the—
PENNY: I'm thinking about cancelling.
FLUX: Why?
PENNY: Maybe I don't need it. The diagnosis.

PENNY *tries to work.*

FLUX: You can just go and see what they say.
PENNY: But what if I don't have it?
FLUX: Then you'll know.
PENNY: I don't know how I feel about having it. Or being *labelled* it. I mean, why is it even called that?
FLUX: What do you mean?
PENNY: It's a very leading name.
FLUX: What's wrong with the name?
PENNY: It's got … undertones.
FLUX: Undertones?
PENNY: 'Deficit' has negative associations. Shouldn't a medical diagnosis be neutral?
FLUX: What do you suggest we call it?
PENNY: I don't have a specific suggestion.
FLUX: Anyway, everyone's got it so it doesn't matter.
PENNY: Well.
FLUX: What.
PENNY: That's the other thing, isn't it?
FLUX: What?
PENNY: If everyone has it then surely no-one has it? A medical diagnosis should point out something out of the ordinary. You don't point out a leg unless the leg is broken, which is out of the ordinary from the way the leg should be.
FLUX: Well not *everyone* has it.

PENNY: But enough people do that it's sort of starting to feel like everyone has it, right?

FLUX: Or maybe people have better access to being diagnosed.

PENNY: Sure.

FLUX: Which is good, now you can actually go and get help that makes it easier to do your job or be in a social setting or go to the bank or supermarket.

PENNY: I can go to the bank. And the supermarket.

FLUX: I don't mean *you* you. I just mean …

PENNY: We should get back to work.

They work.

I just don't understand how it's *everywhere* now. That's all.

FLUX: I think we're just *seeing* it everywhere.

PENNY: When I was getting a referral from my GP for a specialist, she said, 'do you know this suburb does the most referrals in the entire state?'

FLUX: Is that per capita? Or because your suburb's densely populated?

PENNY: That's not the point.

Why are … we … all gathered in one specific area like cattle? Does the suburb appeal to us, or has it caused the symptoms?

FLUX: I don't know if the suburb is related. Causally.

PENNY: But my suburb is why I have symptoms.

FLUX: I don't understand.

PENNY: I'm like this because of my … suburb. Because of what it needs me to do, what it needs me to be. But everything I do to survive my suburb is a symptom.

What if I … changed my suburb?

FLUX: You could.

PENNY *forces herself to keep working. She forces herself to work very hard. She does the thing she does.*

They work.

Do you remember when you were a kid?

PENNY: I don't remember. I feel like I got by fine. So maybe I don't have it.

FLUX: You can go to the appointment anyway.

PENNY: One hour.

One hour to present a specialist with symptoms I've been collecting like supermarket vouchers, so I can cash in for my preferred diagnosis. Symptoms I've specifically curated to exchange for a label.

FLUX: Not a label. A tool. And maybe medication. If that helps.

They work.

PENNY: Apparently it's a developmental disorder.

FLUX: I guess? I don't actually know.

PENNY: I read it. But what happened to neuroplasticity of the brain?

FLUX: What about it?

PENNY: The brain isn't—doesn't have to be this, forever. It can change. It's designed to keep changing. We're designed to keep learning.

FLUX: Sure.

PENNY: So why don't we change our brains instead of medicating it? Why is the solution just chemicals? What are those chemicals even for?

FLUX: To make it easier. For people.

PENNY: To do *this*.

FLUX *doesn't know what to say.*

I feel like an animal at the zoo who isn't behaving correctly and now I'm being put to rights.

FLUX: You're not.

They work.

You're more like … an animal who got so good at using your feet that no-one noticed you had two broken arms. But now you can set your broken arms and it'll be easier to climb the walls. And leave the suburb.

PENNY: Maybe.

They work.

People used to think disease happened because *we* were sick—the body reflected our moral failures back as illness.

FLUX: This isn't your fault.

PENNY: No. But there was a moment we believed that was true.

FLUX: Sure.

PENNY: And now we believe it's genetic. Hereditary. So my daughter—
FLUX: It's not so bad. I know it's scary but it's really not so bad now. People don't see it as a bad thing.
PENNY: Then why do we keep trying to *fix* everyone who has it?

They can't work.

FLUX: I think someone who exhibits none of these symptoms would be incredibly dull to be friends with.
PENNY: That's kind.
FLUX: You don't *have* to take the medication. It's just an option. If you find it helpful.
To get through the work day.
It's not about … you.
It just—might help. With work.

WORK SPACE 4

There's more.

FLUX: It's too much. This is way too much for us to get through.
PENNY: It's fine.
FLUX: We can't. This is—
PENNY: We're fine. We *can*.

They work.

We have to.
FLUX: Hey, have you had your appointment?
PENNY: Let's just get through this.

They work.

FASCIST

FLUX *gets a bunch of phone notifications.*

FLUX: Oh my god.

PENNY *tries to keep working.*

Oh my god.

PENNY: What?

FLUX: Attempted shooting. Another CEO.

PENNY: Who?

FLUX: Some guy in banking. No, tech. No, defence. Sorry, this article is really confusing.

PENNY: Did he—you know.

FLUX: Die?

PENNY: Yes.

FLUX: No.

PENNY: Oh. Good.

FLUX: Is it?

PENNY: Isn't it?

FLUX: The gun jammed and the shooter got shot in the head by security. And then he pissed himself.

PENNY: Security?

FLUX: The CEO. That's why everyone's talking about it. Because he pissed himself. Kinda funny.

PENNY: Is it?

They keep working.

I can't believe it.

FLUX: What?

PENNY: That it keeps happening.

FLUX: It's baseline normal for them at this point.

PENNY: I suppose.

FLUX: But somehow still not—you know.

PENNY: What?

FLUX: Not him.

PENNY: Oh. Yes.

They stop.

Do you really think someone would?

FLUX: What?

PENNY: Shoot him.

FLUX: Fascists get shot all the time.

PENNY: That feels a bit far.

FLUX: Is it?

PENNY: I wouldn't call him a—

FLUX: Wouldn't you?

They work.

PENNY: Maybe he'll just drop dead. He's not getting any younger.

FLUX: Heart attack.

PENNY: Stroke.

FLUX: Runaway bus.

PENNY: Cancer.

FLUX: Too slow.

PENNY: Do you think him dying will change things?

FLUX: Not really.
Killing Hitler didn't hurt the war effort though, did it?

PENNY: … Hitler killed himself.

FLUX: What?

PENNY: When he realised he'd lost the war, he killed himself.

FLUX: Shit.

PENNY: Didn't you know that?

FLUX: I mean, probably. I think I forgot.

PENNY: You forgot?!

FLUX: Look, I'm just saying, lopping off Louis the Sixteenth's head didn't end the monarchy but it didn't *not* end the monarchy, did it?

PENNY: People have tried.

FLUX: I'm surprised there isn't an assassination attempt every two weeks.

PENNY: Maybe there is.

They stop.

Would you do it?

FLUX: If we had guns?

PENNY: If we had guns, opportunity, motive.

FLUX: I think anyone would do anything, with all three of those at their fingertips.

PENNY: Sure, but *really?* You'd risk being found, arrested, shot—

FLUX: I think if things got bad. If things got so bad your back was up against a wall and there wasn't any option left, if it felt like we'd tried everything and we had no choice.

PENNY: You think that's where they are?

FLUX: That's what it feels like.

PENNY: I guess.

FLUX: It's not how it feels to you?

PENNY: I don't think about it much. And if enough of them felt that way someone would have done something by now. Wouldn't they?

FLUX: Maybe it's difficult to get enough people feeling like their backs are against the wall at the same time. It's hard enough getting through the day to day.

PENNY: And people have to work.

They work.

I think it's probably good. That they don't all just go out and shoot him, shoot each other.

FLUX: Even though he's killing people? Even though his actions are literally killing people?

PENNY: Do we want to live in a world where we just *shoot* each other when we don't get what we want?

FLUX: I guess I feel like that *is* the world we live in.

PENNY: So we shoot their people. They shoot ours. Then we shoot theirs. And so on and so forth?

FLUX: Sometimes somebody has to shoot Hitler.

They don't work.

PENNY: I'm just glad we don't have to think about that kind of thing here.

FLUX: Not everyone can choose to not think about it.

PENNY: You'd do it, wouldn't you. You'd shoot him.

FLUX: I think I want to think I'd be brave enough to. But I think I'd just end up being the kind of person who tells people that I wish someone, anyone, someone else, would shoot him. Or whatever version of him we got.

PENNY: Ah.

FLUX: Yeah.

Do you think you would?

PENNY: Oh. Yeah. Absolutely.

FLUX: You're just saying that.

PENNY: No.

We probably shouldn't be talking about this.

They work.

FLUX: Maybe we should.

TRADE

FLUX *almost falls asleep mid-task.*

PENNY: Flux!
FLUX: Shit. Sorry.
PENNY: Were you—
FLUX: I'm fine, sorry, won't happen again.
PENNY: Didn't sleep well?
FLUX: As well as I could on a lumpy couch.

They work.

Not that I'm not grateful to my friend's lumpy couch. I am.
PENNY: It's not ideal. Or comfortable.
FLUX: No.
PENNY: So you and your partner …
FLUX: Ex. Yeah. I've applied for a couple of places but … If it's not too expensive then it's too far away or too mouldy or too party. You know?
PENNY: Sure.

I mean, not for a while, thankfully. But yes.

They work.

FLUX: You know about that guy who swapped a paperclip for a house?
PENNY: That can't be real.
FLUX: It is. He started with a paperclip which he swapped for a pen which eventually became a snowmobile which eventually became a snow globe which became a film role which he traded for a two-storey farmhouse.
PENNY: What's his name?
FLUX: We could do that. Everyone could start with a paperclip and end up with a house.

They work. FLUX *works fast and slightly furiously.*

Money isn't even real anymore.
PENNY: Tell that to my daughter and the sustainably farmed biodynamic vegetables she likes.

FLUX: It's impossible. The number of hours you have to trade in for enough to get a house. It's unreal.

PENNY: Feels real enough when the bank calls.

FLUX: I just wish I could do something that could get me a house.

PENNY: Isn't that what you're doing right now?

FLUX: Something less—this.

They work.

Do you own your house?

PENNY: Excuse me?

FLUX: Sorry. I just—sorry.

They work.

PENNY: Almost.
I almost do.

They work.

PENNY *hands* FLUX *a paperclip.*

You're doing great.

FLUX *stares at the paperclip.*

WORK SPACE 5

There's the same amount.

PENNY: It's been harder to finish everything lately. Do you think?
FLUX: Feels the same for me.
PENNY: I just thought—I *know* now, why it was hard. I thought things would become easier.
FLUX: It's always been this hard. For me.
PENNY: Okay.
Maybe knowing made it worse.
FLUX: Maybe.
Don't you have to go soon?
PENNY: I'm nearly through.

They work.

PTSS

PENNY*'s phone rings.* PENNY *ignores it.*

PENNY: It was awful. I didn't have time to cook so I grabbed a roast chicken from the supermarket and next minute she was screaming about climate change and the oceans and how many chicken bones they would find in a million years and then I was screaming at her and it just.

It was really bad.

It stops ringing. She checks it.

The older she gets, the more she knows, and the worse she gets.

FLUX: It's sad. The things she's learning are sad.

PENNY: And she wants me to be sad with her. But I can't. The psychologist says it might be '*pre-traumatic stress disorder*' and I said if she's got it then surely we all have it?!

FLUX: Maybe we do.

PENNY: What's the point?

FLUX: Of being stressed?

PENNY: Of being *so* stressed? I mean, we're all worried but we can't give in to that.

FLUX: What if the stress makes us want to do something about it?

PENNY: Sure.

But it's all a bit too late, isn't it.

FLUX: I don't think so.

PENNY: No, right. Well.

FLUX: If you've already given up—

PENNY: I haven't given up. I just think the scale of the problem is out of my hands. Or my daughter's. We have to keep going, don't we?

FLUX: Maybe we shouldn't.

PENNY: Then quit.

FLUX: Me?

PENNY: *This* isn't exactly—

Environmentally sustainable.

FLUX: It's not that bad.

PENNY: It's not great.

FLUX: I need this job.

PENNY: Exactly.

I keep telling her it's not our fault, that she needs to be resilient, that we can't fix everything, that I can't fix everything, then she calls me a climate denier but I'm trying, I'm trying to switch to an electric car, and in the meantime we sort our recycling and avoid plastic and do Less Meat Monday but—

FLUX: Meatless—

PENNY: Sorry?

FLUX: It's—don't worry—

PENNY: I don't know how to help her feel like we're allowed to exist in the world imperfectly.

PENNY*'s phone rings again.*

FLUX: She's just scared of the future.

PENNY: So am I.

The phone stops ringing.

PENNY *works.*

LUNCH 3

A delivery of treats.

PENNY: But why?
FLUX: Maybe they're showing their appreciation. For all of our work.
PENNY: But we're …

They're behind. They're quite behind.

FLUX: Isn't this a good thing?
PENNY: There was cake before the last set of redundancies.

They stare at the treats.

I think we should get back to work.
FLUX: Okay.
PENNY: I don't think we should eat it.
FLUX: Okay.

PENNY *works.*

FLUX *quietly slips some of the food away.*

COLLECTIBLE

They're distracted.

PENNY: How many do you have?

FLUX: A few.

PENNY: Why are they so popular?

FLUX: People like them.

PENNY: I heard people queue around the block and fight over them.

FLUX: They don't *fight* over them.
Maybe the limited-edition ones.

PENNY: Limited-edition?

FLUX: Normally they come as part of a series, all in different colours. But they're all packaged the same so you don't know which one you're getting. And there's a bonus colour. So when you buy a box, you don't know if you're going to get a normal one, or a bonus one. It's exciting.

PENNY: False scarcity.

FLUX: Real scarcity. Real rarity. They can get expensive. People sell them online; it's an entire secondary market.

PENNY: It's like gambling.

FLUX: It's not gambling.

PENNY: You put money in, you don't know what might happen. You could get something you don't like, or you could get something you can resell for … How much?

FLUX: A couple of hundred.

PENNY: Wow.

FLUX: I'd sell it if I got one.

PENNY: But you haven't got one.

FLUX: I'm not really trying to.

They work.

PENNY: Does it feel like you've wasted your money?

FLUX: You always get *something*.

PENNY: Have you gotten multiples?

FLUX: Sometimes.

PENNY: Do you sell them?

FLUX: No.

I just like opening the box.

PENNY: How often do you buy a new one?

FLUX: Once a month.

Sometimes more.

It's like a reward. A little treat for working hard.

PENNY: Weren't you saving for … ?

FLUX: They don't cost much.

PENNY: Right.

FLUX: It's nice to get something, you know? I put them on the shelf and it distracts from the paint peeling off the walls.

PENNY: How's the new place?

FLUX: It's fine.

It's this or records or those little lamps everyone's obsessed with.

PENNY: Every generation finds a new thing to waste money on.

FLUX: It's not a waste.

PENNY: They'll be landfill eventually.

FLUX: All of this will be landfill eventually. *We'll* all be landfill eventually.

PENNY: My mother used to collect beautiful saucers and teacups. She was obsessed with them. She didn't even like tea.

FLUX: They're comforting.

PENNY: Everyone loves collecting.

FLUX: Do you have one? A collection.

PENNY: No.

TIME

PENNY: Do you think maybe this is unreasonable?
The amount of—consistency. Of output. That we're expected to produce.

FLUX: Oh yeah. For sure.

PENNY: And we just do it.

FLUX: Yep.

PENNY: Right.

They work. It's half-hearted.

FLUX: Hey.
You're on the slow-release one, right?

PENNY: Sometimes it feels like a placebo. Like I'm committing to focussing.

FLUX: Can I have one?

PENNY: I'm not sure.

FLUX: I've had them.

PENNY: Um—

FLUX: You're not liable. Don't worry.

PENNY: They just make me feel a bit … You know?

FLUX: I could use a little placebo.

FLUX *takes one.*

PENNY: Apparently attention span is a real issue. For everyone, not just kids.

FLUX: Yeah.

PENNY: I can't remember the last time I read a book.

FLUX: I listened to an audiobook recently.

PENNY: Did you like it?

FLUX: I loved it! It was about this girl who went on a train but the train never stopped at any stations and then she—

PENNY: She?

FLUX: I can't remember.
Did I finish it?

They work. Well. They try to.

This sucks.

PENNY: You know what? It does.

FLUX: Do you think they know?

PENNY: What?

FLUX: How hard it is. Like actually how hard it is.

PENNY: I think as long as it all gets done nobody's thinking about it.

FLUX: Do you think if they knew—maybe they'd give us more time?

PENNY: If they knew what?

FLUX: That you needed more time,

PENNY: Do you think?

FLUX: They have to, right?

PENNY: Maybe. What if they don't?

FLUX: Legally I think they have to. It's a disability. Even if people love making memes about it. They have to make concessions.

PENNY: I don't know if I'm comfortable asking …

FLUX: You deserve to. You've been here forever and you've never asked for anything.

PENNY: I've never taken a day off. Except for mandatory leave, I'm always here.

FLUX: Yeah! I'm sure you can ask.

PENNY: I should tell them what I need.

FLUX: Because they don't know.

PENNY: Because I haven't told them. Because *I* didn't know.

FLUX: But now you know.

PENNY: Okay. Why not? Why not!

PENNY *starts to log in to the portal.*

FLUX: No dot.

PENNY: No dot.

Okay. Which of these dropdown options … Personal, organisational …

FLUX: Organisational. No, personal. No, organisational. Because the organisation has to—right?

PENNY: Well, it's a personal request.

FLUX: I guess.

PENNY: I'm going to say personal.

FLUX: Okay! Good idea.

PENNY: And—submit.

SURGERY 2

FLUX: What if I'm just relying on medical intervention to achieve an aesthetic I can't achieve myself?

PENNY: What's wrong with that?

FLUX: But why do I want to look like that?

PENNY: Why *do* you?

FLUX: It's easier. There's a certain way of looking that will make the world, strangers, treat me the way I want them to.

PENNY: Well it is easier. Isn't it? There's an easier way to look. For everyone.

FLUX: Is it wrong to want to enjoy that?

PENNY: You're allowed to.

FLUX: But if I do, then I'm saying I accept that. I accept that there's a right way to be accepted.

PENNY: It's not wrong to want to feel accepted.

FLUX: But why like *that*? Why can't I just be accepted like *this*? Why do I have to change?

PENNY: Will it make you happy?

A long silence.

FLUX: When I think about how much it is.

How much we've raised, collectively, for each other.

Like it's great, it's really so great because people are getting something they otherwise would never be able to get so they can feel the way they deserve to feel.

But the money.

What else could we have done with all that money?

And there's always another fundraiser, one more fundraiser and what if I can't reach enough people? What if people don't love me in specific enough and abstract enough ways to contribute? What if not enough people love me with that kind of money?

PENNY: How much do you need?

FLUX: More.

The bank offered me a credit card.

PENNY: Is that a good idea?

FLUX: I've never had one before.
PENNY: I don't know if it's the best idea.
FLUX: What else am I supposed to do?

STRIKE

FLUX *is working.* PENNY *is on her phone.*

PENNY: God.
It's so awful.
Have you seen this?
About the babies. And the children.

FLUX *barely glances up.*

FLUX: And the adults.
PENNY: Yes.
It's awful.
FLUX: Yeah.
PENNY: I can't believe it's just here. All here.
FLUX: Streamable twenty-four-seven.
PENNY: You know about the—
FLUX: Everyone knows.
PENNY: Not everyone.
FLUX: People talk about it all the time.
PENNY: But I think a lot of people don't *really* know.
FLUX: They should. It's there. All there, all the time.

FLUX *gestures at* PENNY*'s phone.*

PENNY *starts working.*

Everyone knows.
And we don't do anything.
PENNY: We're not doing nothing.
FLUX: Feels like that.
PENNY: It's hard to know what to do.
FLUX: I went to the sit-in at the Minister's office. And the protests.
PENNY: It's hard to get into the city on the weekend.
I should take my daughter.

FLUX *stops working.*

FLUX: They called a strike last month.
PENNY: Who?

FLUX: One of the peace organisations. They said, everyone, for one day, please, just stop. No more until the stock market is in freefall. No more until they stop the killing. The torture. The bombs. No work until they hold guns to your head to start again. No work even then. No work until …

PENNY: Until everything stops.

FLUX: Until everyone knows and it stops.

PENNY *stops working.*

PENNY: I didn’t hear about it.

FLUX: They didn’t get a lot of traction.

PENNY: You didn’t join the strike?

FLUX: No.
I had to work.

They work.

WORK SPACE 6

There's so much. There's so goddamn much. There's no way they're ever going to get through this. How is anyone supposed to get through this?

REVIEW 2

FLUX *is already working.*

FLUX: Morning.

PENNY: Morning.

FLUX: Slow start.

PENNY: I was upstairs.

FLUX: They got back to you about your request?

PENNY: Yes.

FLUX: And?

PENNY: No.

FLUX: What?

PENNY: They said no.

FLUX: They didn't.

PENNY: They did.

FLUX: Just no?

PENNY: They said. That they are sympathetic, and they welcome any adjustments I need to make to my personal routine. But that unfortunately due to their high expectations of their employees and the rigorous demands as to the quality of the outcomes—it's a no. They said no.

FLUX: I can't believe it.

PENNY: They said find another job if you can't do this one.

FLUX: They can't say that. That's discrimination.

PENNY: Well. They didn't say *that*.
But it's what they mean.

FLUX: That's fucked. That's really fucked.

PENNY: We'd better get back to it.

FLUX: No, that's not right.

PENNY: It's fine.

FLUX: It's not. We should stop.

PENNY: We should stop wasting time.

FLUX: We should refuse to work.

PENNY: I just want to do the job and go home.

FLUX: I'm not trying to be difficult—

PENNY: But you are. You are *being* difficult even if you're not trying to be. You're *making* this difficult.

PENNY *works.*

FLUX: They have to change how they do things. They *should* change.

PENNY *works.*

All of this is bullshit. I don't know why we bother coming in every day, doing this over and over again if they're going to—

PENNY *works.*

How can you stand it? All we contribute is waste. Waste of time of resources of our selves—

PENNY: Everything contributes. Everyone contributes. I get it. You feel like you're working too hard, this can't be it, why doesn't it end rent and petrol and insurance and milk and eggs and honey and having to buy the latest jeans is it skinny now, skinny or high-waisted or boyfriend or mum, I can't keep up but it's simple, it's so simple, this *is* it, you just show up and do the thing and show up and do the thing and do it again and again and again and it doesn't matter who you are because we just have to do it. We don't get to stop. You and me, we don't get to stop.

FLUX *goes back to work.*

There's a very long silence between them as they work.

FLUX: There was a slot.

PENNY: Sorry?

FLUX: The clinic called and said someone dropped out and asked if I wanted the slot and I said yes.

PENNY: Your surgery?

FLUX: Yeah.

PENNY: So you've got it. You've got a date.

FLUX: Yeah.

PENNY: When?

FLUX: Soon. Sooner than I thought.

PENNY: Congratulations.

FLUX: Thanks.

PENNY: So you did it. You saved enough.

FLUX: No.
PENNY: Oh.
FLUX: I got it. The credit card.
PENNY: Oh.
FLUX: It'll be okay.
PENNY: I—
FLUX: It'll be okay.

ACT THREE

WORK SPACE 7

There seems to be less work. Or they're getting through it better. Faster.

PENNY: Can you pass me the—

FLUX *does.*

FLUX: Is that the—
PENNY: Yes.

They work.

WORK SPACE 8

FLUX *and* PENNY *work.*

PENNY *takes a pill.*

They're a very efficient pair.

They're getting through it. They might really get through it. All of it.

CALL HOME

PENNY*'s phone rings.*

She hesitates.

She picks up.

PENNY: Hi.
Why wouldn't I?
Well, I'm—on a break.
Soon.
Yes, I remember.
I do listen, actually. The silken tofu. And the cashews. Right?
Don't nag.
Yes, of course the yeast.
No, I did forget. Why don't you text me the list, love? I'll get it on the way home.
Soon.
Okay. Love you. Bye.

She hangs up.

FLUX *doesn't say anything.*

They work.

I'm nearly done for the day I think.

FLUX *works.*

You?

FLUX: I'll just finish this.
PENNY: You don't have to.
FLUX: I'm almost done.
PENNY: You should go home.
FLUX: You're so efficient.
PENNY: So are you.
FLUX: I'm sorry I used to be so slow. So stupid.
PENNY: You weren't. Just forget about it.
FLUX: Don't wait. You have to get home.
PENNY: Don't you?

FLUX: I will.
You should go.
PENNY: Are you sure?
FLUX: You're going to be late.

PENNY *hesitates.*

PENNY *goes home.*

WORK SPACE 9

FLUX *works alone. Late at night.*

WEEKEND 2

PENNY *starts finishing up.*

PENNY: I think I'm finished for the week.
FLUX: Enjoy your weekend.
PENNY: Any plans tonight?
FLUX: No.

PENNY *hesitates.*

You? Any plans?
PENNY: No.

FLUX *works.*

Well.
FLUX: Well. Goodnight.
PENNY: Goodnight.

SHIRT

PENNY *arrives.*

FLUX *is asleep at their desk.*

PENNY: Flux?

FLUX *wakes.*

I didn't mean to scare you. Did you … sleep here?

FLUX: I guess. Sorry, that's so embarrassing. I'll just—one sec.

FLUX *digs out a clean shirt from somewhere and quickly gets changed, tucking the old shirt away. They also do a quick smell test of themselves before applying deodorant.*

They turn back to PENNY.

All done.

PENNY: Have you been sleeping here?

FLUX: No.

Not all the time.

PENNY: But you leave.

FLUX: It's not a big deal.

PENNY: I watch you leave.

FLUX: I do.

Sometimes I come back.

PENNY: Why? You've been getting through it. *We've* been getting through it.

FLUX: Sometimes it's easier. Than going home.

PENNY: But—

FLUX: They don't need to know. About me staying late. Right?

PENNY: Of course not.

FLUX: It's my time. I get to spend it how I want.

PENNY: Of course.

They wait. Uncertain.

PENNY *tries to do the thing she normally does.*

FLUX *fidgets with their shirt.*

PENNY *stares at* FLUX.

FLUX *doesn't look at her.*

FLUX: It's all shirts, isn't it?

PENNY: I beg your pardon?

FLUX: What you said. It's true, everything's just a bunch of shirts.

PENNY: I said that?

FLUX: It's like … you have a shirt. And you like the shirt. You're happy and content with your shirt. Everything is as it should be. You've had the shirt for a long time, it goes with the things in your wardrobe and you and the shirt, you've seen some situations together.

But … Is this it? Is this it for the rest of your life? This shirt that's starting to sag in the shoulders, that's fraying at the edges. Other people get new shirts all the time and they seem happy. They seem better. Why stagnate? Why let yourself get trapped by your own shirt?

You try not to listen.

But sometimes you look at other shirts in the window. And then you see it.

The shirt.

The new shirt isn't like your old shirt. The new shirt is exciting. The new shirt promises that you don't have to stay the same. The new shirt whispers that staying the same might kill you. The new shirt knows you're sad, a little depressed, struggling to sleep at night, but it can fix you. You can fix you. You can look better, feel better, be better.

You ignore it.

You don't need a new shirt. In fact, the new shirt is too good for you.

But maybe … Maybe you deserve it.

You start saving up for the shirt. You start exercising so the shirt will look good on you. Working towards the new shirt feels good.

And then finally, you do it. You buy the new shirt.

The shirt is the best thing that's ever happened to you. It makes you feel like you, but a better you. The real you. You've done it. You've finally found the best shirt.

This is the only shirt you'll ever need. None of your past shirts have ever been as good as your new shirt, you're going to die in this shirt you're gonna die a happy person in this shirt.

Then the shirt gets a little stain on it.

You still love it. You love it even more. Right?

But that little stain under the collar and the armpits makes it look like you don't shower very often even though the stain clearly states that you should shower more. The shirt you used to feel so good and sexy and hot in now makes you look bad, look slovenly, look sloppy, you can't wear the shirt out, you can't wear the shirt, how could you, why would you?

You hate the shirt.

You hate the shirt so much.

You look at old photos of the shirt. The shirt was so pure, so good, so perfect. It could've been your forever shirt.

But there is no forever. There is only the next shirt. And the next shirt. And the next shirt. And the next job. And the next payslip. The new meds, and rent and petrol and insurance and milk and eggs and honey and rent and having to buy the latest jeans is it skinny now, skinny or high-waisted or boyfriend or, and then a house maybe maybe maybe or a paperclip, but definitely another shirt and the next shirt and the next shirt but—

There's always going to be a better shirt.

PENNY *kisses* FLUX.

I cancelled my appointment.

PENNY: What?

FLUX: The surgery. I cancelled and pulled my name. I'm off the list.

PENNY *thinks about reaching out to* FLUX *again. She can't.*

PENNY *leaves.*

EXIT

FLUX *alone.*

They work.

They stop.

They stare at where PENNY *used to work.*

They keep working.

They stop.

They keep working.

They stop.

They look at the exit.

They open the door.

They turn off the lights.

And the world opens up.

LIE FLAT

Somewhere else. PENNY *is lying down.*

FLUX: You never came back.
Why didn't you come back?
I was waiting for you.
I couldn't do it without you.
I—
I missed you.
I didn't think I would, but I missed you.

PENNY: I missed you too.

FLUX: Why didn't you come back?

PENNY: I thought I needed to lie down, that if I spent some time on my own, it would stop.

FLUX: What would?

PENNY: Everything. Or that it would become easier. That it would become easy.

FLUX: Did it?

PENNY: No.

FLUX: So why didn't you come back?

PENNY: Lie here? With me.

FLUX: Are you listening to me?

PENNY: Yes.

FLUX: Penny, I'm trying to talk to you.

PENNY: I had a dream last night.
You were in it.

We were on a boat, a rickety old thing we borrowed from where it was docked by the river. The boat was so alone, we gave it company.

We were there together. it was early, so early in the morning that we hadn't gone to bed yet.

And I was talking to you, I can't remember what about, something so important that it wasn't important at all, and then you were so gentle, you put your finger on my lips and you pointed behind me, and I turned and behind these beautiful mountains was the most orange sun I'd ever seen, coming up between those peaks faster than I'd ever seen a sun come up, we were on the edge of the world watching the sun chase us.

It was the orangest thing I've ever seen.
And I was not afraid.
Will you lie down?

FLUX *lies down next to* PENNY.

They hold hands.

Blackout.

THE END

NEXTSTAGE

Commissioned and developed through Melbourne Theatre Company's NEXT STAGE Writers' Program with the support of our Current Playwrights Giving Circles.

NEXT STAGE positions new Australian works as contenders on the national stage, through strategic investment in stories that reflect our community, are relevant to our times, challenge the boundaries of theatre making and fuel the cultural conversation.

Thank you for sharing our passion and commitment to Australian stories and Australian writers.

PLAYWRIGHTS GIVING CIRCLE

Thank you to Melbourne Theatre Company's Playwrights Giving Circle – its donors, foundations and organisations – for sharing our passion and commitment to Australian stories and writers.

Tony & Janine Burgess, Fitzpatrick Sykes Family Foundation, Jane Hansen AO & Paul Little AO, Larry Kamener & Petra Kamener, Susanna Mason, Prudence & Neil Morrison, Helen Nicolay, Pimlico Foundation, Tania Seary & Chris Lynch, Craig Semple, Dr Richard Simmie, Andrew Sisson AO & Tracey Sisson, Derek Young AM & Caroline Young

Melbourne Theatre Company

BOARD OF MANAGEMENT

Chair
Martin Hosking
Deputy Chair
Leigh O'Neill
Tony Johnson
Larry Kamener
Katerina Kapobassis
Suzie Miller
Chris Oliver-Taylor
Tiriki Onus
Anne-Louise Sarks
Craig Semple
Professor Marie Sierra

FOUNDATION BOARD

Chair
Craig Semple
Deputy Chair
Jane Grover
Karen Cusack
Charles Gillies
Sally Lansbury
Anne-Louise Sarks
Rupert Sherwood
Tracey Sisson

EXECUTIVE MANAGEMENT

Chief Executive Officer & Artistic Director
Anne-Louise Sarks
Executive Producer & Deputy CEO
Martina Murray

ARTISTIC

Artistic Administrator
Olivia Brewer
Associate Artists
Jean Tong
Mark Wilson
Head of New Work
Jennifer Medway
New Work Associate
Zoey Dawson

CASTING

Casting Director
Janine Snape
Artist Engagement Coordinator
Daphne Quah

PRODUCING

Senior Producer
Stephen Moore
Producer
Jess Burns
Company Manager
Julia Smith
Deputy Company Manager
Blaze Bryans

DEVELOPMENT

Director of Development
Rupert Sherwood
Annual Giving Manager
Meaghan Donaldson
Philanthropy Coordinator
Charlotte Menzies-King
Business Development Manager
José Ortiz
Business Development Coordinator
Jahnavi Shivakumar

EDUCATION & FAMILIES

Director of Education & Families
Jeremy Rice
Learning Manager
Nick Tranter
Education Content Producer
Emily Doyle
Education Coordinator
AD Chakraborty
Deadly Creatives Project Officer
Emma Holgate

PEOPLE & CULTURE

Director of People & Culture
Joanna Geysen
People & Culture Business Partner
Maddison Ryan
Receptionist
David Zierk

FINANCE & IT

Director of Finance & IT
Rob Pratt
Finance Manager
Andrew Slee
Assistant Accountant
Nicole Chong
IT & Systems Manager
Michael Schuettke
IT Support Officer
Darren Snowdon
Payroll Officer
Julia Godinho
Payments Officer
Harper St Clair
Building Services Manager
Adrian Aderhold

MARKETING & COMMUNICATIONS

Director of Marketing & Communications
Chris MacDonald
Head of Marketing
Claire La Greca
Marketing Campaign Manager
Aayushi Parikh
Program Marketing & Activation Lead
Rebecca Lawrence
Producer – Industry & Audience Initiatives
Laura Harris
Digital Engagement Manager
Jane Sutherland
Digital Coordinator
Harrison Buikstra
Lead Graphic Designer / Art Director
Kate Francis
Graphic Designer
Sarah Ridgway-Cross
Head of Communications
Isabella Ramdhanie
Communications Manager
Tilly Graovac
Publicity Consultant
Good Humans PR

PRODUCTION

Director of Technical & Production
Adam J Howe
Senior Production Manager
Michele Preshaw
Production Manager
Margaret Murray
Production Administrator
Alyson Brown
Production Coordinator
Zoe Rabb
Technical Manager – Electrics
Allan Hirons
Technical Coordinators – Electrics
Nic Wollan, Max Wilkie
Electrics Workshop Supervisor
Marcus Cook
Production Technician
Ounie Witherow Aitken
Production Technicians & Operators – Casual
Max Bowyer
Stella Dandolo
Claire Ferguson
Isaac Grubb
Sidney Millar
Gemma Rowe
Technical Manager – Staging & Design
Andrew Bellchambers
Production Design Coordinator
Jacob Battista
Props Coordinator
Jess Maguire
Head Mechanist
Tobias Chesworth

PROPERTIES

Properties Supervisor
Geoff McGregor
Props Maker
Colin Penn

SCENIC ART

Scenic Art Supervisor
Colin Harman
Scenic Artists
Alison Crawford
Colin Harman
Nellie Summerfield

WORKSHOP

Workshop Supervisor
Andrew Weavers
Deputy Workshop Supervisor
Simon Juliff
Set Makers
Sarah Hall
Nick Gray
Philip De Mulder
Peter Rosa
Welder
Ken Best

COSTUME

Costume Manager
Kate Seeley
Costume Cutters
Jocelyn Creed
Lyn Molloy
John Van Gastel
Costume Cutters – Casual
Emma Ikin
Costume Buyer
Carletta Childs
Millinery
Phillip Rhodes
Costume Hire
Liz Symons
Costume Maintenance – Casual
Jodi Hope
Claire Munnings

STAGE MANAGEMENT

Head of Stage Management
Whitney McNamara
Resident Stage Manager
Oriana Papa
Stage Managers – Casual
Morgan Clyne
Haydon Dickie
Zsuzsa Gaynor-Mihaly
Mercedes Gowlett
Juliette Hirons
Rain Iyahen
Annah Jacobs
Jess Keepence
Jenny Le
India Lively
Jessie McGuigan
Tom O'Sullivan
Lucie Sutherland
Pippa Wright

CRM & AUDIENCE INSIGHTS

Director of CRM & Audience Insights
Jerry Hodgins
Database Specialist
Ben Gu
Data Analyst
Sionna Maple

CUSTOMER EXPERIENCE & COMMERCIAL

Director of Customer Experience & Commercial
Brenna Sotiropoulos
Head of Customer Experience
Jessie Phillips
Ticketing Services Administrator
Hannah Flannery
VIP Ticketing Officer
Michael Bingham
Education Ticketing Officer
Mellita Ilich
Subscriptions & Telemarketing Team Leader
Peter Dowd
Events Manager
Mandy Jones
Southbank Theatre Operations Coordinator
Drew Thomson
Box Office Supervisor
Darcy Fleming
Box Office Duty Supervisors
Julie Leung
Jessica Pearson
Box Office Attendants
Stephanie Barham
Tanya Batt
Britt Ferry
Casey Gould
Min Kingham
Julia Landberg
Brigid Meredith
Michael Stratford Hutch
Lee Threadgold
Rhian Wilson
House Supervisors
George Abbott
Tanya Batt
Matt Bertram
Zak Brown
Kasey Gambling
Abby Hampton
House Attendants
Rhiannon Atkinson-Howatt
Stephanie Barham
Emily Busch
Briannah Borg
Zak Brown
Sam Diamond
Liz Drummond
Leila Gerges
Hugo Gutteridge
Abby Hampton
Michael Hart
Elise Jansen
Kathryn Joy
Natasha Milton
Ernesto Munoz
Brooke Painter
Lucy Pembroke
Brigid Quonoey
Taylor Reece
Solomon Rumble
Sophie Scott
Mieke Singh Dodd
Ayesha Tauseef
Olivia Walker
Rhian Wilson

SOUTHBANK THEATRE

Production Services Manager
Frank Stoffels
Lighting Supervisor
Geoff Adams-Walsh
Deputy Lighting Supervisor
Tom Roach
Sound Supervisor
Joy Weng
Deputy Sound Supervisor
Will Patterson
Fly Staging Supervisor
Adam Hanley
Deputy Fly Supervisor
Callum O'Connor
Stage & Technical Staff – Casual
Jon Bargen
Suzy Brooks
Connor Brown
Sam Bruechert
Jake Burger
Emily Campbell
Steve Campbell
Will Campbell
Bryan Chin
Harrison Cope
Gideon Cozens
Bryn Cullen
Kit Cunneen
Max Evans
Nick Eynaud
Mitch Forde
Mitchell Forden
Justin Gardam
Alex Giroud
Carla Grcic
Spencer Herd
Ethan Hunter
Marcus Macris
Alexandre Malta
Terry McKibbin
David Membery
David Murray
Sharna Murphy
Alix Otenstein
Jack Palmer
Marco Pezzimenti
Daniel Price
Jake Rogers
Jared Ross
Gemma Rowe
Taishah Simcox
Nathaniel Sy
Tom Vulcan
Dylan Wainwright-Berrell
Darcy Ward
James Williams
Nathaniel Zienow-Sy

OVERSEAS REPRESENTATIVE

New York
Kevin Emrick

Our Donors

We gratefully acknowledge the ongoing support of our leading Donors.

LIFETIME PATRONS

Acknowledging a lifetime of extraordinary support.

Rowland Ball OAM & The Late Monica Maughan
Pat Burke
Peter Clemenger AO & The Late Joan Clemenger AO
Greig Gailey & Dr Geraldine Lazarus
Jane Hansen AO & Paul Little AO
Allan Myers AC KC & Maria Myers AC
The Late Biddy Ponsford
The Late Dr Roger Riordan AM
Maureen Wheeler AO & Tony Wheeler AO
The Late Ursula Whiteside
Caroline Young & Derek Young AM

ENDOWMENT FUND DONORS

Supporting Melbourne Theatre Company's long-term sustainability and creative future.

Leading Gifts

Jane Hansen AO & Paul Little AO

$50,000+

John Higgins AO & Jodie Maunder
Martin & Loreto Hosking

$20,000+

Prudence & Neil Morrison
Andrew Sisson AO & Tracey Sisson

$10,000+

Helen Lynch AM & Helen Bauer
Jennifer Darbyshire & David Walker
Charles Gilles & Penny Allen
Ian Hicks AO
Tony & Nathalie Johnson
Tania Seary & Chris Lynch
Craig Semple

PLAYWRIGHTS GIVING CIRCLE

Supporting the NEXT STAGE Writers' Program, our industry-leading commissioning initiative.

Tony & Janine Burgess, Fitzpatrick Sykes Family Foundation, Jane Hansen AO & Paul Little AO, Larry Kamener & Petra Kamener, Susanna Mason, Prudence & Neil Morrison, Helen Nicolay, Pimlico Foundation, Tania Seary & Chris Lynch, Craig Semple, Dr Richard Simmie, Andrew Sisson AO & Tracey Sisson, Derek Young AM & Caroline Young

TRUSTS & FOUNDATIONS

The Gailey Lazarus Foundation

Annual giving

Acknowledging Donors whose recent gifts help enrich and transform lives through the magic of theatre.

Current as of January 2026.

BENEFACTORS CIRCLE

$50,000+

Krystyna Campbell-Pretty AM
Peter Clemenger AO
The Helen Fraser Giving Fund
Jane Hansen AO & Paul Little AO
Martin & Loreto Hosking
Craig Semple
Andrew Sisson AO & Tracey Sisson
Maureen Wheeler AO & Tony Wheeler AO

$20,000+

Tony & Janine Burgess
Fitzpatrick Sykes Family Foundation
Petra & Larry Kamener
Suzanne Kirkham
Prudence & Neil Morrison
Tania Seary & Chris Lynch
Orcadia Foundation LTD

$10,000+

Alan & Mary-Louise Archibald Foundation
John & Lorraine Bates
Jay Bethell & Peter Smart
Michael Buxton AM & Janet Buxton
Angie & Colin Carter
The Cattermole Family
Karen Cusack
Ann Cutts
Jennifer Darbyshire & David Walker
The Dowd Foundation
Christine Gilbertson
Charles Gillies & Penny Allen
Linda Herd
Daryl Kendrick & Leong Lai Peng (Betty)
Helen Lynch AM & Helen Bauer
Susanna Mason
Helen Nicolay
Pimlico Foundation
Catherine Quealy
The Reid Malley Foundation
Lisa Ring
Dr Richard Simmie
Rob Stewart & Lisa Dowd
Tintagel Bay P/L
Ralph Ward-Ambler AM & Barbara Ward-Ambler
Anonymous (2)

$5,000+

Joanna Baevski
Bagôt Gjergja Foundation
James Best & Doris Young
Deanne Bevan & Guy Russo
M & J Blythe
Bowness Family Foundation
Dr Douglas Brown & Treena Brown
Nan Brown
Dr Andrew Buchanan & Peter Darcy
Ian & Jillian Buchanan
Bill Burdett AM & Sandra Burdett
Pat Burke & Jan Nolan
Diana Burleigh
Alison & John Cameron
S Capp
S Crowe
Prof Glyn Davis AC & Prof Margaret Gardner AC
Andy Dinan & Mario Lo Giudice
Marian Evans
Patricia Faulkner AO
Diana & Murray Gerstman
Heather & Bob Glindemann OAM
Roger & Jan Goldsmith
Lesley Griffin
Jane Grover
David & Lilly Harris
Tony Hillery & Warwick Eddington
Bruce & Mary Humphries
Ian & Titania Henderson Foundation
Amy & Paul Jasper
Alex Lewenberg
Martin & Melissa McIntosh
Libby McMeekin
George & Rosa Morstyn
The Louise & Martyn Myer Foundation
Tom & Ruth O'Dea
Leigh O'Neill
OneTomorrow Charitable Fund
Dr Kia Pajouhesh (Smile Solutions)
Bruce Parncutt AO
Renzella Foundation
Jeremy Ruskin & Roz Zalewski
Lynne Sherwood
Gordon & Faye Shinewell
Janet Whiting AM & Phil Lukies
SALT Catalyst
Price & Christine Williams
Anonymous (8)

ADVOCATES CIRCLE

$2,500+

Ian Baker & Cheryl Saunders
Jenny Barbour
Paul & Wendy Bonnici & Family
Jenny & Lucinda Brash
Bernadette Broberg
C Christian
Geoff Cosgriff
Susan Dahn
Ann Darby
Megan Davis
Kaye & John de Wijn
Pam Durrant
Melody & Jonathan Feder
Anna & John Field
Rosemary Forbes & Ian Hocking
Nigel & Cathy Garrard
The Mary Elinor Harris Fund Endowment
Lording Family Foundation
Colin & Helen Masters
Heather & Simon McKeon
Sandra Murdoch
Nelson Bros Funeral Services
Dr Paul Nisselle AM & Sue Nisselle
Roger & Ruth Parker
Christopher Reed
John & Veronica Rickard
Margaret Sahhar AM
Scanlon Foundation
Dr John Sime
Geoff Steinicke
James & Anne Syme
Frank Tisher OAM & Dr Miriam Tisher
Liz Tromans
The Ray & Margaret Wilson Foundation
Tony & Gillian Wood
Anonymous (3)

LOYALTY CIRCLE

$1,000+

E Abbott & B McComb
Prof Noel Alpins AM & Sylvia Alpins
Julie Andrews
Margaret Astbury
Prof Robin Batterham
Sandra Beanham
G J Bibby
Tara Bishop
Judy Bourke
Nigel & Sheena Broughton
Beth Brown & The Late Tom Bruce AM
Jannie Brown
Lynne & Rob Burgess
Julie Burke
Katie Burke
Geoffrey Bush-Coote & Michael Riordan
Pam Caldwell
John & Jan Campbell
Jessica Canning
F & M Carey
Clare Carlson
Chernov Family
Assoc Prof Lyn Clearihan & Dr Anthony Palmer
Judge Susan Cohen
Sandy & Yvonne Constantine
Deborah Conyngham
Jutta Cowen
Sue & John Denmead
Dr Sally Duguid & Dr David Tingay
J Dunster
Bev & Geoff Edwards
Karen & David Elias
Nita Eng
Anne Evans & Graham Evans AO
Dr Alastair Fearn
Peter Fearnside & Roxane Hislop
Paul & Mary Fildes
Grant Fisher & Helen Bird
Elizabeth Foster
Bruce Freeman
Kerry Gardner AM & Andrew Myer AM
Gaye & John Gaylard
Gill Family Foundation
Fiona Griffiths & Tony Osmond
Ian & Wendy Haines
M D Harper
Luke Heagerty
Gary & Susan Hearst
Lorraine Hendrata
Dr Alice Hill & Mark Nicholson
Brett & Kerri Hereward
Howard & Glennys Hocking
Emeritus Prof Andrea Hull AO
Nanette Hunter
T Johnson
Sally & Rod Johnstone
Lesley & Ian Jones
Michael Kantor
Benny Katz
Leah Kaplan & Barry Levy
Irene Kearsey & M J Ridley
Daniel Kilby
Fiona Kirwan-Hamilton & Brett Parkin
Doris & Steve Klein
Marianne & Arthur Klepfisz
Larry Kornhauser OAM & Natalya Gill
Jane Kunstler
S Lansbury & D Di Fabio
Glenda & Greg Lewin AM
Peter & Judy Loney
Lord Family
Kerryn Lowe & Raphael Arndt
K. Mackinnon
Natasha & Laurence Mandie
Chris Maple
Ian & Judi Marshman
Don & Sue Matthews
Paula McKinnon & Troy Sussman
Garry McLean
Emeritus Prof Peter McPhee AM
Fiona Menzies
Robert & Helena Mestrovic
John G Millard & Andrew Cason
MK Hope
Barbara & David Mushin
Sarah Nguyen
Nick Nichola & Ingrid Moyle
Dr Rosemary Nixon AM
In loving memory of Richard Park
Dr Annamarie Perlesz
Peter Philpott & Robert Ratcliffe
Nathan & Susan Pinskier
Victoria Ponsford
Phil & Gayle Raftery
David Reckenberg & Dale Bradbury
Sally Redlich
Victoria Redwood
Roslyn & Richard Rogers Family
S & S Rogerson
B & J Rollason
Nick & Rowena Rudge
Edwina Sahhar
Alex and Brady Scanlon Giving Fund
FE Scott
Sally & Tim Scott
Jacky & Rupert Sherwood
Diane Silk
Pauline & Tony Simioni
Jan Simon
Jane Simon & Peter Cox
Rachel Slade
Angela Smith

Annette Smorgon
Anthony Steward
Dr Ross & Helen Stillwell
Rosemary Stipanov
Shannon Super
Irene & John Sutton
David & Angela Taft
Rodney & Aviva Taft
Charles Tegner
The Veith Foundation
John & Anna van Weel
Kevin & Elizabeth Walsh
Pinky Watson
Ann & Alan Wilkinson
Robert & Diana Wilson
Mandy & Edward Yencken
Anonymous (25)

SUPPORTER CIRCLE

$100+

Salwa Abdel-Aziz
Jane Allan & Mark Redmond
Lorraine Baker & Peter Hunkin
H & B Bamford
Lawrence Bartak
Jenny Blencowe
Fay Bock
Janet Brasch
Marianne & Robert Broadbent
Dr Christopher & Jill Buckley
Robyn Burke & Graham Burke AO
Anthony & Jan Burn
Elaine Chia & Ettore Altomare
Pamela Chin
Min Li Chong
Mr Peter R Clements
Kate Culbertson
Rosie Cunningham
David & Patricia Davidson
Beverley Davis OAM JP & Dr John Davis
Jenny & Nicholas Dawes
Ruth D
Mary Dyer
Isabel & Graeme Edgoose
Edith Gordon
Geoffrey Grinton OAM & Margaret Grinton
Sally Gudgeon
Katherine Horwood
Rachel & Peter Irons
Dr Michael & Pamela Jonas
Sarah Kimball
Julie Lidgett
Tabitha Lovett
C.N. Luth Esq.
Joy Manners
The Mar Family
Ann McLaren
Glenn & Maureen Monckton
Ruth Muir
Margaret Newton
Helen Oakes
Denis O'Hara & Annette Clarey
Tony Oliver
Dr Hannah Piterman
D Probert
Dr Amanda Reich
Ian Renard
Rock Posters
John Rogerson & Lynette Julian
Andrew Scott
Julie Shelton
Anthony Steward
Ronella Stuart
Diane Tweeddale
Fiona Viney
Sally Wallis
Dianne & Chris White
Richard Zimmermann
Anonymous (146)

EDUCATION GIVING CIRCLE

Alan & Mary-Louise Archibald Foundation
Joanna Baevski
G J Bibby
Judy Bourke
Deborah Conyngham
Geoff Cosgriff
Ann Darby
Luke Heagerty
Larry Kornhauser OAM & Natalya Gill
Heather & Simon McKeon
Christopher Reed
John & Veronica Rickard
Roslyn & Richard Rogers Family
Scanlon Foundation
Gordon & Faye Shinewell
Jane Simon & Peter Cox
Rob Stewart & Lisa Dowd
Ann & Alan Wilkinson
The John & Myriam Wylie Foundation
Anonymous (4)

FIRST NATIONS GIVING CIRCLE

John & Lorraine Bates
Linda Herd
Michael Kantor
Daniel Kilby
Jane Kunstler
Nathan & Susan Pinskier
Christopher Reed
Craig Semple

Thank you

Melbourne Theatre Company would like to thank the following organisations for their generous support.

Major Partner

Future Directors Initiative Partner

MinterEllison.

Major Marketing Partner

The Monthly

The Saturday Paper

Season Partner

Supporting Forum Nights

TIME & PLACE Presents PARK MODERN

Associate Partners

Challis & Company Tomorrow's leaders today

Frontier software Human Capital Management & Payroll Software/Services

K&L GATES

THE LANGHAM MELBOURNE

SCOTCHMANS HILL BELLARINE PENINSULA VICTORIA ESTABLISHED 1982

Supporting Partners

CARGO CREW

COMMUNE WINE

Genovese Coffee

invicium

The Luxury Network

METROPOLIS EVENTS

QUEST SOUTHBANK

southgate

Wilson Parking

Marketing Partners

CINEMA NOVA

RRR

Southbank Theatre Partner

mgc The Melbourne Gin Company

Business Collective Members

Committee for Melbourne

Leadership Collective Australia

Schuler Shook

Current as of January 2026.